Mine is a Community of Misfits & Outlaws

I Write for a Future

*I write for a future
when there is
no moment of dissonance
each time I notice
my expensive pen
of fine design
balanced
in the bony
brown fingers
of a Mexican peasant.*

                                        Jesse James Johnson

Mine is a Community of Misfits & Outlaws

Tenderloin Poetry
by
Jesse James Johnson

Will to Print Press
San Francisco

Faithful Fools and Jesse James Johnson
gratefully acknowledge
support from

Inner Sunset Community Advocates

Without your generous support, the publication of these
poems would not have been possible.
This poetry is but one small example of the art, poetry, and
strength that thrives in the Tenderloin.

Copyright © 2024 Jesse James Johnson

All rights reserved. No part of this book may be reproduced
or used in any manner without the prior written permission
of the copyright owner,
except for brief quotations in a book review
or longer ones to instigate a revolution.

To request permission, contact the publisher at
Fools@faithfulfools.org
or the author at
Jx3sf@yahoo.com

Paperback ISBN: 978-0-9772985-3-2
Library of Congress Number: 2024934718

First Edition Published 2024

Layout/Book Design by Sam Dennison
Edited by Ximena Gasca and Sam Dennison
Cover Art, *El Dividido*, by Lilianna Wilson

Will to Print Press
Faithful Fools
234 Hyde Street
San Francisco, CA
94102
www.faithfulfools.org
@faithfulfools
(415) 474-0508

This volume of poetry is
Dedicated to
Raúl S. Salinas and Linda Ximenes

Foreword

by Tina Valentín Aguirre

We almost immediately became sisters when we met at the 1st National Latina/o Lesbian Gay Organization (LLEGO) Encuentro in Houston in 1992. Under the auspices of talking about HIV prevention, burnout, and frustration with mediocre cultural responses, we found each other as hungry and tired writers and organizers.

We bonded over our mothers. His mom died in a car wreck and my mom survived three instances of cancer.

We bonded over having poet community organizers as mentors. His was Raúl R. Salinas who focused on leftist Xicanismo writings and cultural events. Mine was Rodrigo Reyes who focused on gay Chicano writings and leftist community organizations. We were taught that writing was a means for us to reclaim our identities, narratives and senses when our instincts led us to seek oblivion because of colonization and chaos.

We had nicknames for each other when we lived together. I called him Muerte because sometimes, in the middle of the night, he would walk through the long hallway connecting the rooms in my flat running his nails over the aluminum siding on the lower half of the wall, moaning like *La Llorona*, trying to scare me. I'd say, "Leave me alone, *Muerte, monstra!*" He'd cackle and go back to his room. When I was ready to get up, he'd sing, "Good morning, Heartache" (a Billie Holiday song). It's always been easy for me to say that I'm at peace with death because *Muerte* is my sister.

We both love activism and organizing while rejecting the cult of personality that afflicts many charismatic leaders. More than that, Jesse taught me what he learned from his leftist elders: despite having missions tied to social justice and love, systems and organizations are meant to perpetuate themselves even at the cost of our health and lives. It's a paradox that I didn't believe and understand even when I was deemed disposable over and over again by people and groups I deeply admired and emulated. Jesse reminded me that movements don't depend on specific structures and organizations or even heroes. Instead, we the atoms of change will disperse and reconnect when we can and need to as part of a mobilization for a bigger movement. One project, one group, one leader is not ever going to get us to the next place. We will get there though it's not a straight line getting there.

We were in many writing groups together and I can admit that out of all of us Jesse was, in my mind at least, the best. Still, his relationship to writing is torturous. Sometimes Jesse spent months (years?) working on the same piece and when he finally shared it with me, I'd reciprocate with a poem or a new piece. Often, he asked how long it took me to write and edit it and, on at least one occasion, I let him know that it took me a day, to which he screamed and yelled that he wanted to throw me down a flight of stairs. To this day I consider it a great prize that I earned from him. When he'd write something great, I'd just say *blargh*. In our world, excellence deserves faux shade, probably, because we're just angry and jealous we didn't write it ourselves. Also, we think sheer admiration is too simple (he'd probably say bourgeois).

Today, decades later, I have a huge amount of admiration and love for Jesse and his writing much as I did when we were in writing groups in the 90s. He managed to work on this manuscript despite the resurgence of fascism, the isolation of COVID, and his battle with cancer and the damage to his tongue from the radiation treatment. He also remained active in the Tenderloin serving on boards and working on cultural projects. He still serves as a ghost handler for those of us who still see our dead like the living, we who yell and laugh at the abyss. He is a visionary for our future generations who won't be able to imagine how we survived and thrived during these wars and *plagas*.

For me, all of this is about beauty, love, betrayal and death. And goddamned great writing. Because we deserve fine art, we must have more than revolutionary propaganda, we need poetry and music and creativity that makes sense of everything that doesn't. That we came from dirt, water, air, and fire, and we will return there in a very short time. That we matter and we don't. We live and we die. We love and hate. We are humans and we are monsters.

I've learned that chosen families are important because our biological families sometimes don't have the vocabulary and practice of showing and saying things like "I love you" and "I'm proud of you." It's important that as Jesse's sister I say it over and over again: I love you Jesse and I'm so fucking proud of you! This book is marvelous and, how dare you make something so gorgeous and impactful.

Por siempre, Muerte,
Tu Heartache
Tina Valentín Aguirre

Table of Contents

Tenderloin Poems

Mine is a Community of Misfits and Outlaws	1
Fugitives	4
A Fierce Thirst	5
Joy in the Tenderloin	8
The Colors of Poverty	9
Lito	10
I am Blight and Broken Windows	12
Land of Light, Fog and Mist	13
St. Anne's Valley	14
The Last Monster	15
Poem for the Gentry	16
The Deepest Hours of the Night	18
I Search for Falcons	19

The Long Twilight and Other Poems

The Long Twilight	23
Mother Cosmos	26
Star-gazing	27
Mercury	28
Half-breed	29
The Fiesta Drive-In	30
The March Begins	31

November 10th	32
Jupiter	33
Ozona	34
Pedro	36
Babilonia	37
Mars	39
Life Among the Gemini	40
Washington, D.C. 1979	41
Hiroshima	43
Corpus Christi	45
Monstrous Love	46
Poem for the Last Gay Man Left Alive	47
La Luna	48
Venus	52
Pathway	53
Many Vietnams	54
San Francisco	57
Haiku and Poem	58
AIDS Haiku #513	58
AIDS Haiku #513	58
Xicano Haiku and a Dream	59
Magical Socialism	60
Perhaps Quetzalcoatl	63

Night Spell	67
Railroad	68
Visitors	69
Amsterdam	72
Are We Condemned to Endlessly Orbit?	74
Houston	77
Dreams	79
A Riddle of Scars	80
Prozac Stroll	83
Ama Rita y Olivia	85
Gunshots	87
For the Want of Circles	92
Awaiting the Water	93
Thunderstorm	95
The Great Spirit	96
Changing Worlds	98
Aztlán	100
Earth	101

Introduction
by Jesse James Johnson

    I am heir to a literary tradition that regards poetry as a transformative force. I write for the love of language. I am dedicated to poetry as a craft, seeking those moments when a construction of words crystalizes with insight. When a poem offers even the briefest glimpse into the meaning of life - this is art. Good poetry requires transparency. It requires truth. It is never easy. You risk hurting or confusing the loves you love best. Guilt, stigma, shame, self-doubt, and disapproval must be faced down. To succumb to these forces is crippling. To challenge, to transcend these forces leads toward liberation.

    This book is comprised of two collections: *The Tenderloin Poems* and *The Long Twilight*. The first group of poems are about the Tenderloin district of San Francisco, if fewer it is because they are only the first of what I am sure will be many poems about the neighborhood which has sustained me for almost thirty years now.

    The poems of the second collection were composed over the last 25 years. The Long Twilight is focused not on a specific geographical location but instead is a geography of myth, history, and memory in which the deeply personal and personally relevant intertwine with the cultural and political developments of this country. These poems skim about early childhood events; sweeping through the flowering of identity; the origins of political consciousness; and the discovery of my body and other experiences of young adulthood. They lead to the darker times of my ventures into the wilderness of urban America during the AIDS epidemic. These poems attempt to grapple with living in this period of environmental degradation and its unpromising consequences.

    The Long Twilight did not come easy. It's rare that a poem ever comes to me in one sitting. Some of these poems were long in the making. I could walk for months through the streets spinning a single line of poetry in my head, before a second line followed. Often the third, the fourth or even the last line of a poem could take just as long to emerge. I now realize what I needed was distance, sometimes a considerable distance from the event that inspired the poem. These poems were after about mourning, profound grief and the acceptance of loss.

    It is through the cultural/ideological lens polished in writing this collection of poems that the Tenderloin Poems were written. The Tenderloin District of San Francisco is a vibrant mosaic of ethnicities, languages, faiths, and complexions. It is rich with history and one of the last enclaves of poor and working-class people in the City. The official narrative of the Tenderloin is that of a chaotic, impoverished, deteriorating neighborhood rampant with crime, vice, violence, and drugs; one with residents who are apathetic and of marginal value. Like many urban neighborhoods across the nation, it is under assault by powers that would force out the poor and working class. It would be cleansed of ethnic diversity. It would be redeveloped for the profit and pleasure of the descendants and heirs of those who once swept across this country under the ideological mandate of Manifest Destiny.

The Tenderloin is at once a containment zone, a dumping ground, a refuge, and a sanctuary for socially and economically marginalized and those considered deviant and criminal. I believe the survival of this neighborhood is vital to the future of San Francisco as a city of vibrant progressive thought. And thus, important to the future of the entire country. This is place of new beginnings and second chances. In this neighborhood that disenfranchised people (like those who belong to queer and transgender communities) have historically found a place to discover and articulate who they are. Here, stigma moves toward social justice. Here, criminality and creativity conspire to create a new social consensus. Here, deviance moves toward dissent and then to greater democracy.

I write in defense of this neighborhood. I do so with urgency. For this my home and it is under assault. I struggle to love this place unconditionally. This means giving up notions of good or bad. This means remembering that all humans have value. I love this place. I love the beautiful young peddling drugs. I marvel and at the resilience and strength of immigrant families. I empathize with those who are physically challenged and those who struggle in various conditions of mental health. I long for those students who come here from across the nation to study law across the street from my home to educate themselves about the history of tis neighborhood. I hope that that they might come to understand its value and the power they have to contribute to its survival.

And yes, I love this world we all live in. Even as we enter this period of crisis. Even as we verge on the extinction of millions of species, including our own. I am determined to do what I can to defend this planet. I must believe that we can ultimately figure our way out of this mess. I believe we can collectively make the right decisions to sustain life on this planet. I believe we can build a just society. I don't pretend the future won't be difficult. Nor can I deny that mine has been an amazing life. I am blessed with a warm and loving family (both biological and chosen); I have known extraordinary individuals; I have wonderful and supportive friends and comrades.

Yes, mine is community of misfits and outlaws. We are deviants and transgressors; we are mutations expanding beyond the collective imagination to discover the unimaginable possibilities that lie ahead.

Tenderloin Poems

Mine is a Community of Misfits and Outlaws

I came to this place
almost 25 years ago
my eyes ablaze with crystal meth
a single pair of boots and about 72 t-cells.
This was back when an AIDS diagnosis
meant a quick slide through poverty into a grave.
All I wanted was a room with a door
I could lock against
the voices of my dead friends.

Here we live
the small broken promises
of shattered picture frames
whiskey bottles
mirror shards
cracked ribs
splintered doors
chipped teeth
tattered cosmologies
and zoning laws.
The hubris and debris
of who we might have been
had we not
from the highest
windows jumped
escaping destinies
we could not abide.

I have seen
the poor chew the bones
of those they loved best.
I have seen
the sick stagger about disrobed
in the parking lots of hospitals
begging to be embraced.
I have seen the crippled lying
in hotel rooms staring into space.

The Tenderloin is a place
where the broken, the deranged
and the diseased are warehoused
then left there until their expiration date.
Thankfully, the people have their own notions
about how their lives should be.
They live their lives with defiance
courage and with the freedom
of a people who were never meant to survive.

It is in the despair and capitalist waste
in the ruins of other times
and the fragments of our former lives;
It is in the rot that is the Tenderloin
that we find fecund soil
for our return to the world.

Healing, justice, love, redemption
do not come easy to men.
They require effort
commitment, sweat and humility.
They require a second chance
or a third or more.
No one of us can create
the chance we need alone.
We require the help of others
and we must help them in turn.
Each giving what they can
and only taking what they need.
That is the lesson and gift of solidarity
among the outcast and the poor.

See that woman arguing with her hair?
See her sister feeding pigeons?
Is it prayers they mutter or obscenities?
To me it doesn't matter.

See that panhandler with the homemade sign?
See that young skateboarder sick for heroin?
It is among these, the addicted, the ill
the criminal, the old, the rejected
those who bear the brunt of poverty
those who suffer most the contempt
and violence that America
rains down upon the poor
that I have found shelter, sanctuary
respect, even affection.
Mine is a community of misfits and outlaws.
People who defy convention.
People who transgress borders.
People who push against society's boundaries
and in doing so expand the possibilities
of what the rest of us might be.

Fugitives

The greatest fear of the fugitive slave
is not the hot breath
of the baying hounds
the master's whip
or the branding iron.
The greatest fear
of those of us
who must step out of bounds
is the vast unknown
the yawning abyss
the black thicket of trees
at the edge of the farthest field.

It's the dark tangle
of inner-city streets.
It's the bone cold nights.
The fear of knives.
The dwindling campfires
beneath highway.

It's an empty wallet
a sour stomach
and a padlocked toilet.
It's gasping for breath
in a crowded shelter
where no one knows your name.

It's the wilderness
that is the human heart.
It's the long loneliness
that we must all travel.
It's the fear that this might be
all that sanctuary is.

A Fierce Thirst
Written on the occasion of Hospitality House's 50th Anniversary

A fierce thirst
blistered feet
longing for a deep night's sleep.
To know these things
is to understand
the importance of
being generous with water.
To know these things
is to understand
why a democracy
needs public benches.
To know these things
is to understand
why we dream
of a better time.

This dream is a tree
growing
in a grid of streets
that intersect
with the destinies
of people who
struggle with poverty.
A people generous
and tolerant
with stories of sorrow
and good friends passing
with stories of others
forced out by high prices
with stories of resilience
that defy all predictions.

This dream is a tree
that sprouts
not leaves
but wings
as will happen
when a people are treated
with dignity and compassion.

Their thoughts take flight
they remember a future
long forgotten.
They come to believe
in their ability
to make themselves anew.

This dream is a tree that flowers
in its branches
art
poetry
music
blossom.
Tales of exile and acceptance
stories of injustice and survival
flower
into a mosaic
of narratives
of the Tenderloin
as a kaleidoscope
of languages
beliefs
genders
complexions
and cultures.
(A view of our world
unique and unknown
to outsiders).

This dream is a tree
fruit-bearing
a harvest
of small victories
a job interview
a new pair of shoes
a hair-cut
a room.
Being of value.
Going to school.

Finding strength
among those around you.
Finding meaning
in the struggle.
Finding yourself
in helping others.
Feeling a part of something
larger than ourselves.

This dream is a tree
that grows out of our community.

This dream is a tree
deep-rooted and far reaching.

Joy in the Tenderloin

That day thousands of voices
electric with joy
thundered across
the rooftops of
the Tenderloin.

The streets were flooded
with all our neighbors
addressing one another
as sister or brother
dealing out rounds of congratulations
chuckling with pride
clucking with disbelief
trading jokes
speculating about a future.
Some spoke of miracles.
Some spoke of their sons.

People were dancing.
Boom boxes jamming.
Barbecue grills were fired up.
Someone was handing out
ginger flavored Vietnamese candies
which we all politely took.
There was the sweet smell of marijuana.
Waves of laughter
tears and teasing
admonishments and
much praising
of the higher powers.
More laughter still.
Laughter out loud
and from deep inside.

Of course, there were sirens.
Emergency lights flashing.
Cops revving up their motorcycles
but they kept their distance
until well after dark
the day Barack Hussein Obama was elected President of the United States.

The Colors of Poverty

The colors of poverty
are a shining grey morning
gum wrappers of green foil
a yellow lottery ticket
a fluorescent pink cup
swept into a bouquet
in the gutter.

The colors of poverty
are the violet riot
of an old streetwalker's wig
the turquoise nail polish
of her transgender friend
the Maybelline black
eyelashes
of an Arab store clerk.

They are
copper pennies
in a Mason jar,
ivy growing in a coffee can
a goldfish on the windowsill,
red shoes hanging from a fire escape,
the plastic caps of a used syringe
orange like the flowers of a trumpet vine.

They are the blue velvet
of an R & B song
rainbow colored Buddhist chants
bottles of Big Red
and Purple flavored sodas,
a silver charm.

The colors of poverty are
a dirty saffron colored sky
a smudge of magenta
on the western horizon
a sunset
plum-colored like a bruise
on a young child's arm.

Lito

I am leaning off a fire escape
above the first lights
of evening traffic.
Lito sits in
the windowsill of my room
loading up a pipe
with new stuff
he wants me to try.

"Sometimes I believe
everything is church,
that we are all
infused with the divine.
Sometimes I believe
we all grow wiser
that our perspective grows wider
so that today preoccupations
simply grow too small to concern us."

Lito and I
are accustomed
to these types of conversations.
We find them more comfortable
than having to speak
of anything personal.

Still, he gives me a sideways look
and wants to know
if I have been smoking
something better than the usual stuff.

"While at other times,"
I continue,
"I'm sure
I have never known
anything
of the sacred in my life."

"Maybe not."
He shrugs.

"No worries?" I ask.
"Do you believe God
is going to pass us by?"
There is a hint of anxiety
on his brow.

We smoke
stare into space
neither of us can remember
the last time
we saw a starry sky.

"There is a God,"
he says as he begins
to climb up the fire escape
to his room.
"There has to be."

"Why?"

"Because my mother
is still in Guatemala
and if I could not
entrust her care to God
I might have
to kill somebody."

"Well. He wouldn't want that."

"No," he says.
"So, you see
He has it all worked out.
You've got to have faith
or it all falls apart."

I am Blight and Broken Windows

I am blight and broken windows.
I'm brick walls marred by graffiti.
I'm a row of desiccated trees.

I'm the drug peddler on the hill.
I'm the prophet who stinks of vodka.
I'm the panhandler who demands your money
then calls you a cheapskate
or a bourgeois pig.

I'm a sidewalk altar for an unhoused spirit.
I'm musty pigeons and bloated rats.
I'm a cart of satin rags, busted lamps, and a rainbow flag.

I'm the zombie with rotting teeth stumbling through UN Plaza.
I'm the next-door neighbors' children crying.
I'm *El Cucuy* at the end of the hallway
with a bent syringe and a purple face.

I'm a busted jaw and a beat-up faggot.
I'm five bullet wounds and a missing shoe.
I'm the ghost riding the 19 Polk.

I'm bad art.
I'm the loud and hooting masses.
I'm an advertising major
with an Instagram account.
I'm a can of Drano and a coiled snake.

I'm a black rooster Vudu ritual.
I'm chemo and a dose of daily radiation.
I'm the last defiant Comanche staring at a solar eclipse.

I'm your reoccurring nightmare.

I'm your delusion of escaping to outer space.

I'm a vision of the future.

I'm poverty. I'm anarchy. Embrace me.

Land of Light, Fog and Mist

I have seen these streets in many lights.
In the amethyst cast of an autumn dusk.
In the whitest light of a cloudless dawn.
In the red noon sky of a blotted sun.
Yet, there are mysteries this land still holds.

I might forget that
I live on the ocean's edge
but on this peninsula
there still be deities of the first tribes.
They are the gods of Fog and Mist.

Old lumbering beasts
who roll across the dunes
and pour over the hills
then gracefully filling the valleys
flooding the pools and gulches
and blanketing the rises.
Moonlight adorns them.
There are small explosions
of rainbows if they are touched by the sun.
They shift shapes when caressed by the land.
Here they are a bison, there bear
sometimes serpents.
They stalk the buried waterways
wary as panthers.
They slink through alleys
like a pair of coyotes.
They listen for prayers.
They sniff at the foul air
of this lonely century.

They wonder of those
who once revered them
those who recognized
the sacredness of Fog and Mist
their love of this place
and the role they play in sustaining
life on this land.
Then they turn away
vowing to return one day
to see their kin restored.

St. Anne's Valley

Before the streets of the Tenderloin were laid out, the settlers referred to some parts of the Tenderloin as St. Anne's Valley.

In the ways that water courses
when it rains
the outline of St. Anne's Valley
is revealed.
It is the elegant veined hand
of a giant maiden sleeping
in a gown of sand
beneath Turk and Eddy
in the gulch that sweeps
from Larkin past Mason.
While hovering above
her warrior lover -
dreams in a fallen cloud.

The Last Monster

There is
an apartment building
on Sutter Street
just this side of Leavenworth
and each time I pass it
I am reminded
of a great time
I had there
with seven other men
celebrating
the pleasures of our bodies.
Within five years
after that encounter
four of us were dead
and a week ago I learned
that only I am still in the world.
The last of us.
I am a monster
living in the Tenderloin.

I remind myself
to make them feel proud.

Poem for the Gentry

You have won.
We cannot match
your resources and ambition.
You have won.
We cannot match
your energy and privilege.
You have won.
We cannot match
your desperation and greed.

You look at us and think
we are dangerous and scary.
You might say to yourselves
that we don't deserve this place
because we have let these streets run wild.
But these streets run only as wild as
the passions of the human heart
and we believe there must be room for that.

We might be a crazy bunch of people
but we are close to the Holy Spirit
that is why we can say
you have won
and in that moment not rise in anger
to strike you down.

We are learning patience.
We practice compassion and forgiveness.
Now we are learning to move on.

We have always known that your arrival
would mean our death
but it is hard to imagine not being in this world.
It is hard to know how to move on
gracefully when we have no other place to go.

You have won.
We are leaving.

All the ghosts and birds are leaving, too.
Only the cockroaches and worms
will be here
because they are guardians
and they must remain
even with you.

You have won
but if what you were seeking
is something meaningful
then you have lost.
For if these streets
had something otherworldly
magical even
some power to transform
it is because of the sacrifices
we have made
and we are going.

We leave you not with a curse
but with blessings.
May you be blessed with a sense of history.
May you be blessed with compassion.
May you learn generosity
and a love of truth.
May you be blessed with a consciousness
and with the knowledge
of your role in this world.
May you be blessed with the memory
of who we were
and of what was lost
when we were forced to go.

The Deepest Hours of the Night

There is a sisterhood of trees
that grows outside the Children's Center
off of Ellis and Hyde.
In the summertime
in the deepest hours of the night
these trees fill with the singing
of what birds I know not,
but the music they make is captivating.
Melodic with an almost otherworldly quality.
It's as if the stars themselves
had fallen and swelled
the impenetrably black branches
of these trees with the songs
of those who for heaven long.

I Search for Falcons

I search for falcons
among the high-rises
of downtown San Francisco.

Elegant, winged beings
brushing the borders of extinction
defying predictions of their demise
by reimagining themselves
in the world anew,
bravely building nests
in niches among
the soaring edifices
and mastering the labyrinth of
wind currents
that howl about the high-rises
of downtown San Francisco.

I look for signs-
a dark stroke
across the morning sky.
A distant pair of wings
rising in long trembling swings
twin violins vibrating
among the architecture
of arrogance and raw ambition.

There have been rumors
but no official confirmation
of the return of these fragile constructions
of bone, feather and fierce determination
who each year
fly in an epic migration
across two continents,
one ocean and back again.

Be they immigrants or exiles
the odds are against them.
Their survival as a species
was never guaranteed.

Just as the chances
of my people's survival
is always a question.

I search for falcons
among the high-rises
of downtown San Francisco
what I seek is hope.
A symbol to inspire.
An example of survival
amid these temples built
by those who worship
gold and power.

I search for falcons
embodiments of a savage faith.
Our fates are tied together
we who traveled far
to live here on the edges.
My belief unwavering
that they will return
hurling through the afternoon haze
on winds relentless and unyielding
winging through the downtown canyons
of golden light
screaming their defiance
and heralding the majesty
of the approaching fog.

The Long Twilight and Other Poems

The Long Twilight

1.

I wander
in the Long Twilight
of old anarchists in exile
and gaunt-faced survivors,
of cold jeweled cities
and forests exhausted,
of the buffalo nation's
transfiguration,
of blue-lipped ghosts whispering
remember, remember.

Lonely as a cosmonaut
drifting out of an eastern sky
I miss the Soviet Union
of golden wheat fields
and red sunrises.
Below a geograph of struggle.

Andalusia
    Tenochtitlán
        Guernica
            Santiago
                Soweto
                    San Francisco

Sites of resistance
stand like gentle peaks
on the landscape of history
veiled in mist
wreathed in black ribbons
and the shadows of grief
until evening falls
like a sweet narcotic
to crown the hills in gold and violet.

But, what of Aztlán, *carnal*?
And what was done with Ishi's brain?
Where Quetzalcoatl?

And across the river
the women drum still for revolution.
Lights on the far horizon—
Sputnik, one angry red eye
still blinking
amid the glittering remnants
of Lucifer's hoard,
a ghostly herd
of buffalo,
the smoldering bones
of *El Quinto Sol*
fall cascading
from the planet.

2.

In the Civic Plaza
the last people
lie down
in ordered rows
covering themselves
in hospital sheets
like children
playing ghost
they sleep
still as bread
in meditation.

Until they rise
wave their arms
and bare their fist
in frenzied supplication.
Shallow scoops
of astonishment
forming on their
hooded faces
as they realize
the quiet horror
of Empire's power.

3.

I stand
at the continent's edge
where our histories
crumble into amnesia
asking:
What is to be done?
I go seeking
an alphabet.
Chemicals sparkling
in my brain.
My path
illuminated
by a lung.
I wear
a necklace
of skulls and coins.

From every wire
from every limb.
Ravens enraged
caw.
So much lost.
So much waste.
Too great a price
has been paid
for so little
learned about
the mysteries
of the body.

Mother Cosmos

She is a comet hurling across the sky.

Her thoughts illuminated by
a radium painted dashboard dial.

She wears gold and a peacock blue scarf.

She drives into the late, late night
then takes a turn toward the Great Beyond.

I have yet to say good-bye.

See that red planet? That is the backlight of her car.

Her shattered windshield
is now a halo of glittering stars.

A distant nebula she wears as a shroud.

Her luxurious hair is ever Dark Matter.

I am a small moon.

All Gravity is grief.

Star-gazing

Star-gazing
in my father's arms.
He points to
the Dippers
Winged Pegasus
the Dog Star.
We follow the colored lights
of an airplane ascending.

He begins a story
of their first car trip
south to Matamoros.
They argued about driving.
She wanted a license.
She insisted he stop
by the edge
of the highway
to pick the wild Daises
she believed
St. Margaret favored.

The rumbling plane
disappears into the west.
The immensity of our loss
pours into the bowl
of the sky. Starlight
glistens in his eyes.

When he speaks again
it is of Orion, distance
remembrance, my mother
and the violet crush
of the night.

Mercury

The tooth
held in his fist
falls in a sigh
beneath
the dark wet
lashes of his sleep.

In the blue shadows
of his pillow
the young child
dreams:
Bright orbits
swift wings
of bone and light.

He wakes
to find
a silver Mercury dime
and a small piece of his life
spirited away
by the night.

Half-breed

My mother was Mexican.
My father was white.
After summer days of running around
shirtless, and wearing long pants
my torso was a pecan brown
my legs the color of *masa*.

Standing up in the tub
I proclaimed,
"This part of me is Mexican.
This part of me is white."

"Sit down you're splashing
water all over the floor."
My sister scolds as she pushes me back into the tub.
This must have been before I turned six
because I remember my sister being warned
not to make me cry
which meant this must have happened
while my mother was still alive.

The Fiesta Drive-In

As Hummingbird's gift of fire
ignited the ancient mind with knowledge
the deities *del cine mexicano*
flickering on the giant screen
that filled the night
gifted me with a sense beauty
taught me the value of justice
dignity, honor
and songs that I still sing.

The March Begins

Día de la Raza.
¡Justicia, Trabajo y Libertad!
Stop Police Brutality!
The proclamations
of a black-haired people
took flight
on the fire-red wings
of banners unfurling
in the October sun.

¡Adelante Raza!
The March began.

November 10th

A single image of
blue pills spilling
into my cupped hands
framed in a nimbus
of golden light
is my only memory
of the day I turned 18.

Jupiter

We are leaving
the car is packed - lashed and tied.
It is midnight and hot.
September - still summer.
Shirtless and gleaming with sweat
we wash with a water hose
beneath a majestic Oak.
The house is empty now
quiet as the woods.
Only the windows
want to speak –the screen wires tremble.
The glass panes
mute reflections
like still water
the color of
my father's eyes in the morning.

Ozona

A roadside *jacal*
outside of Ozona.
We buy *cigarrillos mexicanos y Fanta sodas*.

Aquí tocaba
Little Joe
in the late sixties.
Mary Sue's sister
had some great stories.
Locos on the radio waves
(before everyone was busted).
Saturday night *bailes*.
Dusty *jamaicas*.
Dancing circles
of Tex-Mex sounds.
Colored lights
of traveling carnival rides.
An emerging *Raza* consciousness
entre la gente joven.
The nights smelled of
Aqua Net *y mota*.
Our origin myth
was born in
the breath
of an accordion.

An ancestral trail
runs the length
of this desert.
*¿Cuántos han pasdo
por esta tierra?*
Footsteps
in the chaparral.
The great magueys
feed on the waste
of slaughterhouses.
I slash my palm
on an aluminum can.
A wound
that splits
my lifeline.

What is transgression?
What is betrayal? *¿Pisar bandera?*
How long must
I suffer the loss
of my motherland?
What are the borders of survival?

Today
I take another path.
Head west.

I leave the desert
lean and long-limbed.
Lean (requires less water),
long-limbed (to dissipate heat)
like my people a *Cahuileño*
pero caminando
towards the sea.

Pedro

*Desde que
me salí de Tejas
he cargado
esta piedra*
shaped like
a *cabeza.*

He *perdido
tanto
en esta vida
cartas,
fotos,
libros,
anillos*
even the rosary
from my
first communion.

*Milagro que
esta piedra
se ha quedado
como un perrito
pegado conmigo.*

*Esta piedra
me guarda recuerdos.
Esta piedra
es mi tierra.
Esta piedra
se llama Pedro.
A veces, jugando
le digo*
"Peter Texas."
He hates the name.
Se hace el mudo.

*Pobre
Pedro
piedra
cabezudo.*

Babilonia

Yes, the earth is hollow.
The stars unfixed.
Look, Venus is falling into that other sky.
Fathers die.
I can hear all the waters
weeping in a shoe.

Hello? Hello?
We have a bad connection.
Electronic snow.
A chattering like loosened teeth.
Inarticulate, twisted truths
and so much left unsaid.

I am eating horses.
I've lost my reflection in a lotus pond.
My words are wafers
of muck and regret.
Ephedrine flowers in my eyes.

Ay, *peregrino*,
man-child born of
a wedding moon.
Ahijado de la muerte.
You flying into Babylon.

From the cathedral silence
of a midnight airport
 I watch your plane rise.
Sorrow templed in a gleaming box
against a sky
dark with thunder
with lightening enraged. Medusa
ripping at her hair.
Screaming
in madness.
By grief
undone.
Yes!

Yes! The earth is hollow — *y llora*.
But look, hummingbird
brings fire.
And man? Men are ...
straw
salt
lava
stone
fear
honor
pride
pain
alchemy.

Mars

Mujeres. Indians. Faggots. Whores. Young black men. Junkies. Vets. Baby girls in Asia. The Children of Abraham. Africans. The mentally ill. The people of East Timor. The poor. The poor. The poor.

Life Among the Gemini

I live among the Gemini / twins who sleep / in a twist of limbs / speak in riddles / and love / in knots of hallucinations / I hear many voices / water nymphs in the toilet bowl / conjured friends / psychiatrists / hallways whispering the wrong directions / holy apparitions weeping/

I go walking / seeking solace in / the noise of traffic / and still they call / from mailboxes and passing cars / from the windows in the canyon walls / from every rooftop / in the Tenderloin/ I am sick of them / I hate their voices / be they oracles or schizophrenics / they flood my ears with lamentations / mindless gossip / and conspiracy theories about alien races/

They grab at my clothing / urge me to follow / as they descend into the sewer tunnels / but a mind can be lost and not recover / from the dark embrace of the underground/ I pull away / stick to the sidewalk / I concentrate on neon signs / and traffic lights / refusing the seductive whispers / of Hades and valium/

Exhausted / I light a cigarette / exhale / and settle on the concrete steps / of an entryway/ guarded by Chinese dogs/ Soon enough / a woman steps up around me / to rattle the gates that bar her way / screaming / let me in / the sky is heavy / I need my pills/

As her demands echo away / a glassy silence stands to replace them / she rattles harder / strong as an orangutan / I'm impressed / but the well-lit hallway remains impassive / I offer her a cigarette / no thanks she says / not my poison / I can tell/ she wants to cry/

I step away / I've decided / to walk down Polk St. / then cruise by the park / after that / I'll give it up/ I go spinning a poem in my head / hoping to will away / the two headed demon / that springs out of the night / when grief is twinned with desire / and madness grows wings / takes to the sky / singing an aria / to the dead / I drag behind me/

Washington, D.C. 1979

*For Ramón, Blackberri and all those who attended the first
Third World Lesbian and Gay Conference held in 1979.*

I hear the echoes of protest
and I think of old friends.
Thundering chants
reverberating
in the streets of
downtown
remind me of
a march
of red and orange
splotched leaves
in a purple rain.

We were in
Washington, D.C.
for a march.
I remember
breezes
off the Atlantic Coast.
A rain had fallen
that afternoon
the streets
were silver-black
and traffic yellow
the buildings were grey
and copper green.
Beneath the eaves
pigeons squabbled
like Trotskyites.

We believed
in revolution.
Buying books
was a great pleasure.
That evening
we heard
Audre Lorde speak
and something new
in us emerged.

A year later
would come
the election
of Ronald Reagan
with a soundtrack
of boots on the horizon.
AIDS stalked us
like the Terminator.

The end began
of course
you died
and what
began in us
was diverted.

My memory
plays tricks on me
I hear
dogs barking
and believe
them to be
the echoes of protest
of old friends
marching.
I remember still
the faith we shared
in the power
of transformation
in the belief
that whatever
we've become
we can
begin
anew.

Hiroshima

> *For D.Y. who many years ago left us on the anniversary of the bombing of Hiroshima*

At Octavia and Grove
three Ficus trees.
I am astonished at how high
these trees now reach.

How long has it been
since that mist-veiled night
when I hid beneath
these tangled branches,
in fear, in jagged grief,
in crystal madness,
to watch a window
where my friend
was dying?

I am astonished at how high
these trees now reach,
at the swirling white blossoms
that fall from their crowns.

Is it snowing in Hiroshima?
Do the hills still sleep under twilight's blue shroud?
Does the mist still gleam with ice and uranium?

Some wounds do not heal.
Not all is forgiven.

How long have I stood
a blind pillar of salt
unable to step forward,
to bear witness to
your body's rough passage
into the big sleep?

How long must I winter your death;
live with this festering curse,
this coward's mark, this wound, radioactive?
My temples grow white now,
my bones are soft as tuber roses.

Perhaps I, a coward, remain
but I have grown wiser
and so less afraid.

I am astonished
at how high these trees now reach
as I walk under
their vaulted branches
to cross the street
and stand beneath that window.

Not seeking your pardon
but that I might be near you.

For mine is a splintered heart,
that will always mourn you
and yet still beat
without the
forgiveness of the dead.

Corpus Christi
Standing on the seawall of Corpus Christi, Texas, looking out the Gulf of Mexico, three months into the BP oil spill.

A late freeze
and six Ecuadorian roses
are worth more than
a peasant's bloodied fist.

There is a rebellion of elephants
in Indo-China.

A Palestinian child
dreams of plutonium.

They are shooting coyotes
in Golden Gate Park.

Birds fall out of the sky.

Frogs are dying faster than homosexuals.

Whales have abandoned the Sea of Cortez.

Please, stop.
Step out of your car.
Behold your body.

Pelicans drift
at the edge
of the water.

Monstrous Love

3am
I find comfort
in the measured breathing
of my companions sleeping
in the queer blue light
of a blank video monitor
on the living room wall.

Two, like reclining twin Buddhas
on my roommate's new sofa,
one sprawled out in an easy chair,
another wrapped in a rug on the floor.
They are a landscape of Cedar and caverns.
They smell of tar and an old hunting jacket.
They taste of electricity and salt.

Ours is a monstrous love
fueled by the fat hunger of faggots,
and pornographic images
that flicker hot on the tube.
Evoked by that unnamable power
that summoned
out of turbulent, defiled, radioactive waters
Godzilla—to rage, breathe fire,
and avenge the long years
of his solitude.

Yes, he is vile, perverse, an abomination.
Yet, I find comfort
in his misshapen head,
clawed ugly feet and blood-shot eyes.

As I have found comfort
in this cluster of men.
For they are as serpents amid
the leaves and figs.
They are nights of sand.
They are a watchtower.
They are a thunder of gargoyles.
We are a hideous bride.

Poem for the Last Gay Man Left Alive

Should you be as Ishi,
the last of your tribe,
Hide.
Shield your eyes
from gems and electronics.
Embrace your loneliness.
Eat maggots if you must
but remember this -
Priests, cops, psychiatrists and Ph.Ds.
are the enemy.

They are pollution.
They will smile and stroke
your confusion.
They will fondle your brain
as a pervert might a little girl.
They dissect dreams.
They profit on ghosts and bones.
They want to trap our spirits in a book.
.
They will claim to want
to help you find us.
But we are gone.
You must remember this.

Should you be as Ishi,
the last of our tribe,
Hide.
Hunt only at night.
Find one who might love you.
Tell him our names.
Whisper them
like nasty curses
as you fuck in the dark.

La Luna

The Stars.
The Stars are a bunch
of shiny-faced punks
mean as a pack
of coke-addicted Siamese cats.
But even though the odds
are like a zillion to one
against her
they won't mess with *La Luna*.

The Stars
while not as bright
as they might look
are still not dumb.
They know *La Luna*
just a middle-aged *ruca*
from the Eastside.
Unmarried. A life-long *soltera*.
She has no family
to speak of
except for her *hermano* - *El Sol*
an ex-military type who lives
on the "better" side of town.

Still, they sense *La Luna*
has no fear of them.
They don't know why.
This confuses them.
So, they make themselves scarce
when she comes around.
They'd rather spend their time
on easier prey
like maybe a white dwarf
or one of those comets
with a fancy tail.

What the stars don't know
is that *La Luna*'s
glow of confidence,
her swag, her *firme* stance
the way she breaks out
her signature moves
as she dances across the Milky Way
is all because *La Luna* secrets
a loaded pistol
in the inner pocket of her jacket.

She knows there are
treacherous currents
in the depths of the sky.
Every night she sees
Chained Andromeda
Medusa beheaded
Coyolxauhqui
hacked into a hundred pieces
among the constellations
that move in solemn procession
against the dome of heavens.
She is determined
that will not be her fate
and so, she is packing heat.

It's her talisman against fear.
Her skeleton key to the cosmos.

A gun in a man's pocket
is a dangerous object.
It spits death.
A gun in a man's pocket
can be more stupid
than a hard prick.

But a gun on a woman
is an amulet
with powers far beyond
the force of the bullets
that sleep in its womb.

La Luna says the gun
allows her to do her job
without fear of harm.
She can conduct
her nightly rounds
without having to worry
about the nasty little stars
or some lecherous drunk planet
weaving through the sky
making suggestive comments
as she passes by.

It means she can wear a gown
of lacework and platinum
or one of stardust
hot clouds of plasm
without consequences.
It means she can linger
to enjoy cool ocean breezes
and apply the scented oil of her choosing.

La Luna says
a gun let's her
powers shine
so she may comfort
the homesick
console star-crossed lovers
inspire poets, artists, late-night disc jockeys
and whisper secrets
to spell-casters and farmers.

It lets her make the clouds shimmer
brighten landscapes
flood urban canyons
and fill dark alleys with light.
So, we who must travel these paths at night
need not always stumble through dangerous shadows.

When she flies just above our heads
trailing moonlight like gentle caresses
we pause, look up
and from beneath our dark hoods
give our thanks.
For She is the guide.
She is the reflected light.
She is the power
that pulls on the blood of bodies
ever west to the end of our journery.

Venus

The Blue Lady sings
a song sorrowful
as Palestine
sweet chariot
fall.

You are
a meteorite
striking
through the pines
the brush
of a cotton sheet
falling from
a body
at sleep
intimate
and cold.

You are
the pale
light
of morning.
You are
mist.

Pathway

Distance.
Breath.
Letter.
Wing.

Root.
Rafter.
Family.
Tree.

Shadow.
Weather.
Trumpet.
Shoes.

Blood.
Illusion.
Pathway.
Sleep.

Many Vietnams
Let there be not one, not two, not three, not four
but many Vietnams.
                                           Che Guevara

Vietnam 1: On becoming Vietcong

At eleven
we were
tin-can poor.
My body was
a strange country
at war with itself.
I was a stick figure
with the dark limbs
of a Chinaberry tree
and eyes like two machetes
squinting against the sun
with a cannibal's smile.

At eleven
I dug tunnels
climbed trees
scampered about in
guerrilla rags
ducked down alleyways
and the soft dirt paths
of vacant lots
avoiding the enemy.

At eleven
I was effeminate.
Strange as the East.
Vicious as a country dog
I smelled of gasoline.
I was dangerous with fire.
At eleven
The war was everywhere
I watched it on TV
I studied maps
I recognized the flags
I knew which side
was powerful

and which side
was right.
I knew then
I was Vietcong.
The enemy
of bullies
was the side
where I belonged.

Vietnam 2: Shrapnel

Everywhere we find
the legacy of
of the Imperial wars.
The main strip of Aransas Pass
a string of blinking lights
over the back-alley entryway
to the Blue Lotus Massage and Spa.

I am meandering home
smelling of Thai stick and incense
high as a nineteen-year-old.

He is in the driver's seat
of an idling grey Cadillac
one wheel straddling the sidewalk
clenching the steering wheel
his head bow as in prayer.
He radiates danger.
She clutches her red
polyester robe.
Her face is powdered
white as a ghost.
Her black hair glistens with the colors
of the neon signs.
She leans into the car.
She strokes
his thinning hair.

She says:
Come in, come inside.
Just like Vietnam.
I promise.
Just like Vietnam.

Vietnam 3: A chant against despair of the war in Iraq.

Vietnam won!
Vietnam won!
Vietnam won!

San Francisco

When we
from the distant future
look back
on San Francisco

we shall discover
a city of atoms
sparkling with random,
kinetic connections.

and we will remember
 that we were after all
a City of lovers.

Haiku and Poem

AIDS Haiku #513

The ashes of friends
are a tumble of boxes
in my back closet.

AIDS Haiku #1432
Clinical Trials

I don't mind
being a guinea pig
except fortune-tellers
complain
it is difficult
to read
the future
of someone
with such tiny paws.

Xicano Haiku and a Dream

Haiku

¡Perros! ¡Racistas!
¡Marranos y fascistas!
A picket-line chant.

Homesick

When all I dream are *nopalitos*.

Magical Socialism

For Haydée Santamaría.

I want a book of political theory
as beautiful and protean
as twilight waters
of *El Malecón*.

A book of exquisite verses
of crafted rhythms
and charming rhymes
containing metaphors of
transformative power
and images so sharp
they cut to
the pearly surface
of the bone.

A volume of poems
revealing
the conditions
of our lives
the value
of our bodies
labor
reproduction
alienation
capital
economy.

A collection of slogans
protest chants and manifestos
bold and explosive
as the fireworks and banners
that inspire
us to rally
to lock arms
to march forward
to lift our gaze higher.

An almanac
of sonnets
to feed the poor
good meat and peaches.
The Collected Poems of Ho Chi Minh.
Los Corridos de Ricardo Flores Magón
Limericks by Bobby Sands.
Fables from the Holy Land.
The recipes of Ethel Rosenberg.
Psalms for Junkies.
Chants to ignite Ghost Dance.

A disappearing spell for these three words: cunt, nigger, maricón.
A disappearing spell for these three words: cnt, nigr, marón.
A disappearing spell for these three words:
When recited three times.

Page after page
of eulogies
farewells and praise for
(among them)
Allende (*El presidente*)
Malcolm
Amílcar
Nora
Ernesto
Jimmie
Lorraine
Roque
Camilo
Federico
Marsha
Ingrid
Ramón

Y usted, Haydée
Revolucionaria
Héroe
Mártir

Pages of haiku
as numerous as

A chorus of leaves
singing of strange new truths and
old bitter faiths.

The final section
an unfolding
litany of names -
murdered Spanish anarchists
martyrs of the Arab Spring
every woman buried in the borderlands
in shallow graves of sand.

Perhaps Quetzalcoatl

The Morning Star
was murdered
over the jungles of Bolivia.
A firestorm
of lead and lightening
that ripped through
the grey veil of dawn
to forever stain
the eastern horizon with
Quetzalcoatl's spilled light.

Only his body
a cold slab
of tortured flesh
 bullet riddled and
pock-marked
like the moon
is left behind.

A grisly prize
for his Death Squad assassins
the vicious beasts
of a panting Reaction.

For the faithful
only confusion and
questions remain.

Where are the Dodos?
The Condors? The Quetzals?
So much has disappeared.
Whole nations, the ancient codices,
mother tongues, the coral reefs,
Victor Jara's fingers, Democracy,
the sacred trees. Without
the rainforest, how shall we breathe?

Perhaps Quetzalcoatl
ceased being a god
when with his divine vision
he foresaw
that his powers
could not prevent
the contagion.
A sickness
that was to fall
like a plague
of white moths
upon
the walls
of municipal buildings,
eating books,
smothering out
the lanterns of reason,
caressing our hair,
burying their eggs
in our deepest fears.

Our throats choke
with silken scarves.

We speak caterpillars.

Perhaps Quetzalcoatl
is his wisdom
divined
that with faith alone
we could not survive
an invasion of our bodies.

And so
left behind
his human remains.

Perhaps we need
to become
cannibals again.

We'll roast his flesh
to feed ourselves.
Cure his skin
for the leaves of books.
His eyes we'll
raise as burning lamps.
One hand (the right)
will be used in
the healing arts.
The left shall be
a divining rod.
His skull will be
our meeting house.
His thigh bones shall
serve as shovel and hatchet
and from
his finger bones
we'll fashion flutes.

Strand by strand
his hair
we shall release
into the air
to spin
and in the howling wind
combust.

Burn bright
and grow
longer
than the Amazon.

Shining paths
that shall
lead our way
out of this
bitter season of despair.

Beneath bright banners
we shall march
singing praises of our bodies
expelling in our tears
the insects that nest
inside.

Until we stand
in the golden city
of El Dorado
high atop
a volcano peak

and from those heights
we shall see
all the ancient trails
drawn in fire

leaping the spines
of mountain ranges
spanning the Americas
from the ice fields
of the northern lights
to Tierra del Fuego
in the south
where long ago
in a secret grove
the last of the Dodo birds
gathered
to listen
for the end
of the terrible slaughter
and our call
for their return.

Night Spell

Say "Black is beautiful."
Say it loud
and the earth shines brighter
the evening sky
is purple satin
the Milky Way
crushed gardenia blossoms
the bone-colored
crescent moon —
horns of
the Black Madonna.

Railroad

I remember
when black was beautiful.
Men were fine panthers
soft as coal.
Women were sharp
as railroad spikes.
And hope swelling
like a mighty engine
freedom glittering
in its light.

Visitors

We are not strangers
foreigners or aliens.
We are your neighbors
your associates, your friends.
We are your kin sabes
but no doubt intimately related.
Would you too not bleed red
if you opened a vein?
Perhaps you have just failed to notice
much less remember —
but we have been here beside you.
We understand
you have been preoccupied.
We're told it happens
to even the most intimate relations.

Once we have visited a while
all that will change.
No need to worry
it's not like we intend to stay forever.
Still, you won't mind if we use the toilet?
And some of us may have to sleep
beneath your bed, tonight.
The temperature has dropped
and our tents have been taken.
Please don't be alarmed
we won't be in your way
we'll do all our cooking in your hallway.
This will be an occasion to
deepen our acquaintance.

Already we are "connecting."
Your son—so well mannered
for a young man of his age.
He is generous to a fault
and has invited us to make ourselves at home.
He even showed us
your hidden your stash.

Your wife is lovely
if a bit distant
and your dog - oh what a lovely bitch,
so friendly
the beast absolutely adores us.
All she wants is a little attention.
You see, she senses your indifference
and feels unfairly treated.
She complains you favor your children
when she is the more loyal.
Have no worries, it's only routine venting
a little growling under the breath
some bearing of teeth.
You should not fret over any of this.
Let them work it out.
You have other concerns
of which we can be of assistance.
We can help clear up your life
lighten your load.
Let's pull down these drapes
and let in some light.
We can share new ideas.
Open your garage.
Sell your car and teach you to use public transportation.
We can tell you jokes and make you laugh.
How many people in your life can really do that?
We can reveal your ambitions for what they are.
Help control your greed and understand your fear.
We can help ease your foot off the planet's throat
and loosen that fist that grips your heart.
Who doesn't need some assistance
every once in a while?
Some words of support?
A little propping up?
A relaxing stroll to the ATM?
We knew we must help.

We recognized your need
when we wandered by
and saw your toilets
spewing sewage into the streets.
We heard your car alarm screaming
which your wife ignored
as she drove off in the new Tesla.
It was then that we found you
passed out on your front step
clutching an empty bottle
of expensive gin.
If that's not a cry for help
then what is?

Amsterdam

In a bathhouse
waiting for my lover
after a night exploring
the winding hallways
the numbered doors
the pools and reflections
of the human heart.

Discovering
the small insights,
hard truths
and revelations
in the weeds
of brotherly
conversations.

Mesmerized by
the smiling reflections,
the sparks of magnetic
attraction
the play of light
across a lover's brow
in a star-lit pool.

I close one door
to enter another
and in each room
I find
a mirror
a lamp
a single bed
one for every
lover of my past.

The warmth of the body
is a terrible power
it can drive a man crazy
bind comrades together
comfort a lover
allow us to heal another.

All this,
the heart holds chambered,
against forgetting
and the changing seasons.

I close the door
I step outside
to fill my lungs
to clear my mind.
To wait for my lover
with a grateful spirit
beneath the generous sky
of Amsterdam.

Are We Condemned to Endlessly Orbit?

The greybeard
in black leather
and I
are the only
two cruising
Ringgold Alley
tonight.
It's 4:30am.

We speak.
Walk side by side.
I ask,
Are we haunted?
Or are we haunting
a world that is no longer ours?

Are we condemned
to endlessly orbit
the great abyss
that is the loss
of so many comrades?

He smiles.
Yeah, it's dead tonight,
but I'm not a ghost.
I'm flesh and blood
and you seem
to be made
of solid stuff.

He continues.
What is sometimes felt
as an emptiness
is the loneliness
we all share
and of course
the great losses

that we must carry
for the
privilege
of having been
two amid the multitudes
that passed
through places
such as this.

To have been part
of that Great Convergence,
of men who gave
up their bodies
in battalions
to be fused
together by the heat
of that great muscular
power that we are.

That we are? I wonder. Still?
A power...? A collective ...force?

Call it that or whatever.
He answers.
What matters
is that we value
and remain attentive
of the individual connection
that makes us all
an entity larger
than ourselves.

And it's my turn to smile.

As we have been walking
the morning mist
has snaked up
from behind us.

Flooded the alley.
Softened the harsh
glare of the street lights.

He asks me
to his apartment
we move
in that direction
and as we reach
the end of the alley
I can hear
a thousand pair of boots
marching in fog.

Houston

1.

The heat here can kill
a feeble bodied man.
The canals stink
of rot and kerosene.
The crepe myrtles
sway full as the sea.
The evening is sticky
with honeysuckle.
The moon
if she arrives
will do so with
an entourage
of cool breezes.

2.

The Museum District.
I saw 7 sculptures
by Picasso
reality compressed
like a car wreck
in motion.

Headless angels,
horse drawn carts,
whores, domino players,
serpents on fire,
flying dogs
and jazz musicians.
Ink on cardboard
or butcher paper.
The drawings
of an old tombstone carver
buried in a pauper's grave.

Ancient masks, baskets,
fetishes, darts and other treasures
stolen from 18th Century Pacific Islanders.

Mobiles by Calder.

A whole fucking chapel by Rothko.

Figurines crafted in
14th century Tehran.

The art of
3 gay men.
All dead.

3.

The rains of the Gulf Coast
warmed by lightening
wash the palms
of dust and grit.
The afternoons
of sand and clay
smell of blasted glass.
The rage of a hurricane
is a promise
from an angry god.
The screaming Terns and
Egrets take flight.
The geckos scurrying
across puddles
of water
like Christ
hurrying to his fate.

Dreams

1.

I am sometimes so lonely in my dreams
I wake up in tears.
At times I am angry with my father.
Tonight, there was a key I must deliver.
It had a rusty tongue.
I was a subway car
riding through the catacombs.
"*Puros hombres,*" the conductor muttered.
"*¿Y las mujeres?*" I asked
"*Quemadas. Ceniza y polvo.*
Things were different then," he says
pointing to a bullet hole
in the in the back of his head.

2.

I must climb
rusted fire escapes
narrow flights of stairs
steep desolate cliffs
rickety ladders stretching into endless space
in order to get home.
I am terrified of heights.
Sometimes the fear weighs so heavily
I am paralyzed.
I consider just letting go
but tell myself
I'll wake soon, I hope.
Until then, I'll just hold on.

3.

I still dream
of smoking cigarettes.
Eating solid food.
Driving.
Fucking.
Shooting up.
And of long conversations
with dead friends.

A Riddle of Scars

My arms are a riddle of scars.
Exclamation points
and questions marks.
Arcane equations
and mysterious runes
in constant reconfiguration.

Are they dots and dashes that spell a message?
Do they hold the clue
to Rumpelstiltskin's questions?
Are they signs of my transgressions?

Do these scars track a junkie's
stumbling run
in desperate search
of a pumping vein?

I could say these scars are evidence.
They testify against me.
They are markers of my disease.
They are signs of deviance.
But once simple answers
speak only of simplistic truths.

Do these scars mark me
as a heretic
who only prays
when I need a fix?
A penitent
I pierce my flesh
and watch my blood
flower into a syringe.

See that *Chicanito*?
He is carving crucifixes
into his flesh
each cut an Aztec/Catholic sacrament
stigmata wounds
food for the divine

These scars chart my journey
into the wilderness
seeking answers of the mysterious
my vision quest
into the great abyss
attended by Indian ghosts
and scorpions crawling
in the smoke
of landscapes set afire.

They are the stitch marks
of leather threads
used to sew shut
the mouths of shrunken heads
to bind the borderlands
together like a Frankenstein.
A no-man's land that traffics
in human flesh
and chopped up cars.
A burial ground
for our murdered daughters.
A cesspool of industrial toxins.

These scars are pale fish
floating in the waters
of the Rio Grande
a prophetic sign of babies born
with lizard brains
on the border.
These scars are the thorns
of flowering vines
of magueys and chaparral
that grow in dreams
out of my arms.

These scars are hieroglyphic
carvings on an ancient wall.
They warn of the dark god
in this body
templed.

They speak of deep longing
of secret ceremonies
sacred rituals
of wounds and liberation.

These scars are
as puzzling as a Rubric's Cube
one twist of answers
canceling out another
yet all revealing
a common root
that many truths
might exist at once.
These scars ease my loneliness.
They are my legacy
and testament.
They are evidence
of my healing.

Prozac Stroll

Nothing surprising
jumps out of my hands.
They have been wrought of chaos
and a passion for emphasis.
They look waxy and are dumb
as unlit candles.
They won't hold a pen or a fist.

But the floors are well swept
and the books are arranged
according to size.
Nothing surprising jumps
out of my shelves.

We go to the movies a lot
to escape the humid afternoons.

Outside
the day is colored
like a '70's game show.

Why are we talking
about Las Vegas, again, again?

Everything
looks far away
as if seen
through toy binoculars
held backwards.

All the doors
are purple or yellow.

They open and shut
wagging their tongues
like telephones.

Now the windows
fly away.

At the end of the block
(which is a great distance.)
a little man dressed in black
waves a Stetson and shouts:
"Faster, faster. They'll get away"
then disappears
around the corner.

I shuffle forward
as fast as I can.
I want to run
but I'm afraid to lose a shoe.

Let go of my hand, please.

Don't you hear the accordion music?

Please, let go of my hand.

My chest feels like
soggy cardboard.
I can poke my finger
through my heart
without finding its center.

Poems bleed
on my tongue unspoken.

Let go. Let go. Who are you?

Amá Rita y Olivia

Amá Rita,
their grandmother,
argued furiously with her guests;
about Tino's car accident
why she never married by the Church
¿Quién mató a la perra Wiggy?
¿Y qué significaba
un gallo negro en el portal?

While these were
dilemmas long resolved
or mysteries settled
and drained of drama
hace años.
Amá Rita's guests
were ghosts with faulty recollections
and she herself suffered
a profound disconnection
and believed too many memories
only lead to confusion.

So as the past itself was wide open
the historical narrative
contested territory
they mostly applied themselves
to larger questions.
What myths must be passed
to the next generations
or the internal quirks of logic
unique to each superstitious belief.
These were issues which took skill to discern
and meant years of quibbling.
These were debates that drew upon
the wisdom of saints
and even sometimes
the testimony of the serpent itself.

Only two things did not provoke debate.
On only two things
was there uncontested agreement.
The death of the child buried by
Amå Rita buried three quarters of a century ago
in a shoe box in her backyard
was not the fault of any one person
but was the will of a mysterious God.
And the grandson now called Olivia
had always been the way she is.
A mystery to all
but certainly, the creation of a perfect God.

Gunshots

A beautiful afternoon
on Potrero Hill
the sky a sweet blue
air the color of daisies.

We hear gunshots.
We mark the direction.
We gauge their distance.
We each measure the reverberations
until without speaking we judge
ourselves to be safely positioned
and continue.

We don't want trouble.
We are here for a picnic.
We settle in
unwrap our burgers
share French fries
slices of melon
pass around
bottles of water
pop open cans
of still chilled soda.
We offer open hands
to beckon butterflies
to alight on our fingers.
We watch wasps
iridescent as beads of black glass
dance in the long blades
of translucent green grass.
We tell ourselves
that after all
what we heard
might not have been
gunshots at all.

We believe
we are safe
beyond danger's reach
but we are not.

From these heights
we can see
the new sports arena
sleek as a yacht,
gleaming columns of stone and glass.
Fences of steel wire
to keep trespassers out.
A tangle of highways,
housing projects, cranes, steeples
railway depots, schools of old brick
playgrounds, strip malls, auto shops,
row upon row of little box houses
undulating toward
the shimmering waters of the Bay.
Great ships are docked
magnificent beasts, white flanks,
breaking from the sea
poised like Darwin's lungfish
to slide onto land.

Sunlight flashes off
the chrome of rumbling traffic
like signals for help
from drivers choking in
the fumes of their own cars.
And somewhere in that gridlock
of rage and bad choices
a catastrophe
of sound and radiant heat
is exploding
and we hear once more
a series of sick, sharp rapports.
Shots were fired.
Someone is bleeding out
this afternoon.
We hear sirens
ripping through the
exhausted air.

A fire truck,
a pack of police cars
then at a distant third
an ambulance
caught in the snarl of backed up traffic.
We see a pod of young men shatter
one falls beneath
the slow grinding traffic.
The others disappear.
Traffic stops dead
and the site of the wound
opens to reveal itself.

We are numb
with shock, in disbelief.
We told ourselves
we were safe
sitting here in the long grass
and flowering clover
on a hillside
still visited by coyotes
beneath a sky
endless and empty
save for the blessing to two hawks.
How could we have been so stupid
as to think that our proximity
from the violence
meant we were safe?
How could we forget
that the reverberations
of violence
travel far beyond
the point of impact?

It's a question of geography.
For we are one landscape.

This hill
these streets
these power lines
these sisterhoods of trees
the twisted logic of traffic signs
the pattern of windows
reflecting one sky
one moon
one sunset.
We are one.
If we are to survive,
there can be no us and them
no we and the young
no poor and the other
no innocent and not
no we and those
who live in Bayview Hunter's Point.
Those young men in trouble
all the young men of this City
are all our children.
For we are one people
or we are not people at all.

So, if you hear a gunshot
what do you do?
Duck.
Take cover.
Check yourself for wounds.
Don't hide.
Act.
Rush like antibodies.
Render aid.
Give solace.
Rage in protest.
Bear witness no matter the distance
you can testify
if you're willing to stand.

So, if you hear a gunshot
be it in the dead of night

in a sun-drenched park
or on the six o'clock news
you are not safe.
To believe so is delusion.
The distance you feel is only denial.

No matter where or who you are
Remember this:
If you can hear a gunshot
you can take
a bullet to the heart.

For the Want of Circles

The world wants circles.
Serpents and beginnings.
Mandalas and calendars of stone.
Helixes and hoops.
Ripples upon the pond's still surface.
Lullabies undulating on desert sands.
Here the sun will rise.
There the road will curve.

All remains the same
except now, the trees are gone.
So too, the strange bird
like the good grass now burned away.

Awaiting the Water

We walk about stupid
in the ashes of burning forests.
Wondering about
the presence of water
and where the sacred beings,
who would hear our prayers, hide.

The fires
distant in the night
are beautiful.
They are like liquid jewelry
that we vainly
hold to our throats
smiling before grey mirrors
until radiation blisters
in ropes around our necks.

Maybe wise fish
will find a way
into the deep water of caves.
Maybe the darkness has kept
a shield of silent owls alive.
Maybe we can
huddle on rooftops
numb with horror
and somehow escape
the plague of knives
that howls through
the rooms below.

Maybe the day
will again open its eye
smokey with grief
weak and asthmatic
straining to breathe.

Maybe we will discover
a landscape
utterly alien
diminished by greed
covered in ash
but sprinkled with seeds
burst open by fire
awaiting the water
of our tears
and the food
they will leech from our bodies.

Thunderstorm

We are the grandchildren
of the thunderstorm.
We are beings of
water and electromagnetism.
We are the bloodline
of a primal force
distilled through generations.

We are vessels
haloed in light
gifted with a language
with which
we will
one day
speak to stars.
We carry the
secret elixir of the Holy Spirit.
We carry the souls
of all the Long Walks.
We carry the rage
of a planet abused
by fear and greed.
We carry
a longing,
(brief but every returning)
to be water
and wavelength
to be thunder
lightening
burning cloud
primordial howl
and in our joyful power
rain.

The Great Spirit

1.

The Great Spirit
that is the sky
spreads it wings
to conjure a night
ablaze with stars
fragrant with juniper
and the promise of rain.

Gentle wings guide
our journey
over curving black serpents
and magenta sands.

East to where my father
will be buried
at the edge of the southern plains.

2.

We shall all
each through our own journey
arrive
with bare feet and dusty hair
to a field of stone and yellow flowers.

There we wander
among the grave markers
and broken angels
mouthing the names
of ancestors and dead lovers.

The tragedies
and miracles of life
are exhausting.
We grow heavy with nostalgia.

Lower our bodies
to the stony ground.
Close our eyes
and give ourselves
to the cicadas singing
in the broomweed
and yarrow.

We dream.
We dream of purple thistles.

Barking dogs wake
those who must return.

3.

Hiking up hills and along dried arroyos.
I seek the counsel of crows.
I laugh with coyotes.
I burn copal and sage.

When I cross a path
that my father walked
I miss the comfort of his arms.
His absence is a sack of stones.

Mesquite trees tremble
with splendor and thorns.
Leaves swirl.

I am now
an elder of my tribe
and I must face the coming storm.

Changing Worlds

Dear Alanna,

I fell through
the starry crust
of the highest cloud
and was lost in Outer Space
somewhere between
the stormy Asteroid Belt
and the vast plains
of Venusian fires.

This is a crossroad.
A transit point.
Cosmic rays are a tapestry of ghosts
that travel in waves.
The Crab Nebula
flares in my throat.
I wade through Dark Matter.
I watch the Great Karmic Wheel
break through the dark waters.
An orb of burning plasma
that is the sun.
Though I wrestled against gravity
the old Titan, Atlas
and an exquisitely formed angel
given no name.
I was captured by the cycles
of beauty and heartbreak
of love and leave-taking
like a lone wolf
in elliptical orbit
around a female–led pack.

And so, it was
until I heard
Cuco Sánchez singing
and followed
the vibrant lines
of his golden guitar strings
to a village
on the coast of Tamaulipas.

I live there now
in a small house
of stone and tile.
A vine of blue morning glories
adorns my front porch.
Avocado trees
grow in the back.

Every morning
while making coffee
I am ridiculed
by a gang of parrots
because I know
so little of *fútbol*.
(They are *Cruz Azul*.)
I am suspected
of being a *marihuanero*.

I spend my afternoons
combing a post-apocalyptic beach
for polished glass and talismans.
I listen for the turtles' songs.
I watch fishing boats
cast their nets
into the nothingness
as they drift into the south.

Although it's taken me a while
to figure this out
I now realized
this might be my afterlife.
Which explains why
the postcards I send
are always returning
and why the woman
who lives up the hill
is dressed like *La Virgen de Guadalupe*.

        Forever, your loving,
        Uncle Jesse

Aztlán

The
imagined/nation
of *poetas*
and *pintores*.

Blazed across the walls
of housing projects
and up the undersides
of bridges.

But murals fade.
El Pueblo se cansa.

They vanish
like the
ancient Maya.

Strings of
colorful *papel picado*
left hanging
after a celebration
El Viento shreds
into little
palabras.

Hummingbirds
of future
idiomas.

Earth

At noon the cedars are an electric green.
The limestone bluffs a pale yellow.
The water is dark
and sparkles like mica.
Fish breathe.

This book would never have happened without
the inspiration, assistance and/or encouragement of these people:

Jacqueline Johnson-Garza, Fina Sherrie Fabela,
Mary Sue Galindo-Juarez, Maria S. Limon, Leah Laxamana,
Ximena Gasca, Liliana Wilson, Valentín "Tina" Aguirre,
Carmen Barsody, and, of course, Lidia and Cynthia Pérez for their
unwavering faith in my abilities.

**¡Amor y abrazos!
Thank you, all!**